ideals
EASTER

The world itself keeps Easter Day,
And Easter larks are singing;
And Easter flow'rs are blooming gay,
And Easter buds are springing.
Alleluia! Alleluia!
The Lord of all things lives anew,
And all His works are living too.
Alleluia! Alleluia!

John Mason Neale

ISBN 0-8249-1033-8 350

IDEALS — Vol. 42, No. 2 February MCMLXXXV IDEALS (ISSN 0019-137X) is published eight times a year,
February, March, May, June, August, September, November, December
by IDEALS PUBLISHING CORPORATION, 11315 Watertown Plank Road, Milwaukee, Wis. 53226
Second class postage paid at Milwaukee, Wisconsin and additional mailing offices.
Copyright © MCMLXXXIV by IDEALS PUBLISHING CORPORATION.
POSTMASTER: Send address changes to Ideals, Post Office Box 2100, Milwaukee, Wis. 53201
All rights reserved. Title IDEALS registered U.S. Patent Office.
Published simultaneously in Canada.

SINGLE ISSUE — $3.50
ONE YEAR SUBSCRIPTION — eight consecutive issues as published — $15.95
TWO YEAR SUBSCRIPTION — sixteen consecutive issues as published — $27.95
Outside U.S.A., add $4.00 per subscription year for postage and handling

The cover and entire contents of IDEALS are fully protected by copyright and must
not be reproduced in any manner whatsoever. Printed and bound in U.S.A.
by The Banta Co., Menasha, Wisconsin.

Publisher, Patricia A. Pingry
Editor/Ideals, Kathleen S. Pohl
Managing Editor, Marybeth Owens
Photographic Editor, Gerald Koser
Staff Artist, Patrick McRae
Research Editor, Linda Robinson
Phototypesetter, Kim Kaczanowski

*Front and
back covers
HOLLAND TULIP GARDENS
H. Armstrong Roberts*

Easter

Easter, with its voice of Spring,
Ushers in the morning;
'Tis time for earth's awakening,
Time for earth's adorning.

Let church bells sound their chimes
And ring out on the air,
A call to come to worship
And meet the Lord in prayer.

With heart and love ascending,
Your joyful praises sing,
In faith and hope and wonder —
Behold your risen King!

Mrs. Inez Lemke

Photo opposite
CROSS ON HILL
Santa Fe, NM
Ed Cooper

The Light Comes Brighter

The light comes brighter from the east; the caw
Of restive crows is sharper on the ear.
A walker at the river's edge may hear
A cannon crack announce an early thaw.

From the book THE COLLECTED POEMS OF THEODORE ROETHKE by Theodore Roethke.
Copyright © 1953 by Theodore Roethke. "The Light Comes Brighter" Copyright 1938 Atlantic
Monthly Co. Published by Doubleday and Co.

The sun cuts deep into the heavy drift,
Though still the guarded snow is winter-sealed,
At bridgeheads buckled ice begins to shift,
The river overflows the level field.

Once more the trees assume familiar shapes,
As branches loose last vestiges of snow.
The water stored in narrow pools escapes
In rivulets; the cold roots stir below.

Soon field and wood will wear an April look,
The frost be gone, for green is breaking now;
The ovenbird will match the vocal brook,
The young fruit swell upon the pear-tree bough.

And soon a branch, part of a hidden scene,
The leafy mind, that long was tightly furled,
Will turn its private substance into green,
And young shoots spread upon our inner world.

Theodore Roethke

March

Blossom on the plum,
   Wild wind and merry;
   Leaves on the cherry,
And one swallow come.

Red windy dawn,
   Swift rain and sunny;
   Wild bees seeking honey,
Crocus on the lawn;
   Blossom on the plum.

Grass begins to grow,
   Dandelions come;
Snowdrops haste to go
After last month's snow;
Rough winds beat and blow,
   Blossom on the plum.

Nora Hopper

Catkin

I have a little pussy,
    And her coat is silver gray;
She lives in a great wide meadow
    And she never runs away.
She always is a pussy,
    She'll never be a cat
Because — she's a pussy willow!
    Now what do you think of that!

Author Unknown

The Willow Cats

They call them pussy willows,
    But there's no cat to see
Except the little furry toes
    That stick out on the tree.

I think that very long ago,
    When I was just born new,
There must have been whole pussycats
    Where just the toes stick through —

And every spring it worries me,
    I cannot ever find
Those willow cats that ran away
    And left their toes behind!

Margaret Widdemer

From LITTLE GIRL AND BOY LAND by Margaret Widdemer, copyright 1924 by Harcourt Brace Jovanovich, Inc.;
renewed 1952 by Margaret Widdemer Schauffler. Reprinted by permission of the publisher.

The Daffodils

I wandered lonely as a cloud
That floats on high o'er vales and hills,
When all at once I saw a crowd,
A host of golden daffodils;
Beside the lake, beneath the trees,
Fluttering and dancing in the breeze.

Continuous as the stars that shine
And twinkle in the Milky Way,
They stretched in never-ending line
Along the margin of a bay:
Ten thousand saw I at a glance,
Tossing their heads in sprightly dance.

The waves beside them danced; but they
Outdid the sparkling waves in glee:
A poet could not but be gay
In such a jocund company:
I gazed — and gazed — but little thought
What wealth to me the show had brought:

For often, when on my couch I lie
In vacant or in pensive mood,
They flash upon that inward eye
Which is the bliss of solitude;
And then my heart with rapture thrills,
And dances with the daffodils.

William Wordsworth

Spring

The last snow is going,
Brooks are overflowing,
And a sunny wind is blowing
   Swiftly along.

Through the sky, birds are blowing,
On earth, green is showing,
You can feel earth growing
   So quiet and strong.

A sunny wind is blowing,
Farmer's busy sowing,
Apple trees are snowing,
   And shadows grow long.

Now the wind is slowing,
Cows begin lowing,
Evening clouds are glowing
   And dusk is full of song.

Harry Behn

The Wind

I saw you toss the kites on high
And blow the birds about the sky;
And all around I heard you pass,
Like ladies' skirts across the grass —
   O Wind, a-blowing all day long,
   O Wind, that sings so loud a song!

I saw the different things you did,
But always you yourself you hid.
I felt you push, I heard you call,
I could not see yourself at all —
   O Wind, a-blowing all day long,
   O Wind, that sings so loud a song!

O you that are so strong and cold,
O blower, are you young or old?
Are you a beast of field and tree,
Or just a stronger child than me?
   O Wind, a-blowing all day long,
   O Wind, that sings so loud a song!

Robert Louis Stevenson

Easter Bunnyland

These are busy days
In Easter Bunnyland—
The Easter Bunny's helpers,
His furry little band,

Are making nests, painting eggs,
Busy as can be—
Planning Easter goodies,
Sweets for you and me.

Even Grandma Bunny,
Who lives down in our lane,
Helps to wrap the chocolate eggs
In colored cellophane.

Mother Hen sends nice fresh eggs,
Mrs. Cow gives butter—
Eggs are boiling in the pot—
My! things are all a-clutter.

Mr. Bunny helps out too,
For Easter's drawing near,
And everyone will celebrate
In the springtime of the year.

Shh! the bunny's helpers,
Are watching you and me!
They hide among the bushes
Or stand behind a tree.

They are watching now
   as Santa does
For naughty girls and boys —
And if you aren't very good,
You may miss the Easter joys

Of finding brightly colored eggs
The bunny leaves at dawn —
Hidden in the bushes,
All about the lawn.

If you would see this magic land,
Just stand upon your toes,
Cross your middle fingers,
And look along your nose —

There! before your two bright eyes,
Plain as plain can be —
You'll see the Easter Bunny
And all his family.

Richie Weikel

MY BUNNY

I walked down through our garden
One balmy day in spring,
And suddenly I stopped short when
I saw a lovely thing.

A soft and cuddly bunny,
As sweet as one could be!
He'd never heard my footsteps,
So sound asleep was he.

On tippy-toes I ventured
A closer look to gain,
And there I knelt beside him . . .
I scarcely could refrain

From scooping up this bundle
Of downy fluff, but oh,
That moment he awakened . . .
You should have seen him go!

The grassy spot was still warm,
My secret wish had flown . . .
So close I was to having
This bunny as my own!

Georgia B. Adams

EASTER PARADE

On April 9, 1882, New York City hosted a unique Easter Parade. Unlike the legendary Fifth Avenue procession, this cavalcade journeyed up Broadway from Battery Pier to Madison Square Garden, not in holiday sunshine, but in rainy darkness. Instead of beautiful ladies in Easter finery, sixteen horses were featured, as well as two elephants, Gypsy and Chief. More to the point, from a huge crate mounted on wheels, the guest-of-honor trumpeted to cheering crowds: the highly acclaimed Jumbo the elephant had arrived in America!

Shortly after his merger with James Bailey to form Barnum and Bailey's Circus, P. T. Barnum purchased Jumbo for $10,000 from the Royal Zoological Gardens in London. There, for seventeen years, countless British children had ridden happily on his back and indulged him with buns and other delicacies. He was the largest elephant in captivity, standing twelve feet tall and weighing seven tons.

When knowledge of the sale became public, all Britain voiced anger and indignation. School children and editors wrote letters of protest. Londoners purchased "Jumbo" soups, salads, overcoats, hats, neckties, and scarf pins; the money collected was channeled into a special fund for Jumbo's re-purchase. The Fellows of the Zoological Society brought action for a court injunction to prevent the sale of Jumbo. So great was the furor, the *London Fun* suggested replacing the lion on the British coat-of-arms with a likeness of Jumbo and the motto "Dieu et Mon Jumbo."

Eventually, however, the huge crate constructed for Jumbo's transport was positioned amidships in the giant hatchway of the *Assyrian Monarch*, displacing six hundred immigrants to America. Jumbo's British friends provided buns, oysters, and liquid refreshments for his comfort, and the ship signaled news of the elephant's health throughout the voyage.

On Easter Sunday morning, Barnum and Bailey and other dignitaries visited the anchored *Assyrian Monarch* to greet Jumbo. The elephant's crate was hoisted to a small vessel and transported to Battery Pier amidst the cheers of nearly two thousand spectators.

The excitement continued. The difficult task of placing the crate on wheels caused the first delay. And then, there was the mud. When eight circus horses were unable to move crate and wheels, hundreds of volunteers tried to pull the conveyance with long ropes. The two circus elephants, Gypsy and Chief, joined the retinue and pushed from behind. Finally, with the help of eight more horses, the wagon was freed.

More crises occurred. Would there be clearance for the wagon beneath the city's elevated tracks? There was, by a mere two inches! At Liberty Street, the wheels got stuck in earth piled up from steam pipe excavations. Twice, the wagon's axles overheated. Near the Lafayette Statue, a cab driver watching the unusual parade lost control of his frightened horse and caused a general disturbance. Meanwhile, Jumbo trumpeted loudly and swung his huge head from side to side during the chaos he was creating. Finally, late at night, the procession reached Madison Square Garden; only then did it become evident that the horse-drawn wagon transporting Jumbo was too large to fit through the entrance.

Jumbo's controversial sale and spectacular arrival made him a great attraction to the public. Barnum estimated that purchase and transport of the elephant had cost $30,000; Jumbo brought in $336,000 the first six weeks he was on exhibit. Capitalizing on his popularity, American businessmen used the elephant as a symbol in their advertising and promotional campaigns. His trainer, Matthew Scott, published Jumbo's biography for avid fans, and once, as a publicity stunt, led him across the newly constructed Brooklyn Bridge to test its strength. Over four million children and sixteen million adults viewed Jumbo during his American lifetime.

Even after his tragic death in 1885, Jumbo made a contribution to our lives: the use of his name to designate spectacular size. And it all began with the unique and chaotic Jumbo Easter Parade.

Alyce Mitchem Jenkins

Eggcentricity

Mention eggshells to most people and words that come to mind are cheap, common, disposable, fragile, even trash! In the hands of Donna Marie Runge of Menomonee Falls, Wisconsin, however, an eggshell becomes a unique and precious keepsake, a treasure destined to become a family heirloom.

How did the homely egg travel from the hen house to the display case? From antiquity, eggs were decorated and used as gifts symbolizing life or renewal and as an expression of love. Ancient Persians even believed our planet had been hatched from a giant egg and revered the common egg as a symbol of Man's beginnings.

Donna Marie's interest in eggs isn't quite this ancient, but began instead as an outgrowth of a 4-H project. As the leader of twenty-two young people, she was faced with the challenge of creating interesting projects for her charges — a new one each year.

"It started," she recalls, "with a poultry project. One year we raised chickens, another year we studied housing, then grooming for show, then we traveled to shows, then we did different methods of food preparation with fowl. Finally, the only things left were the eggs!"

She and a friend spotted a jeweled egg in a craft shop, signed up for a class and after a two day seminar walked out with their first decorated eggs. Soon, Donna had her twenty-two 4-H'ers (aged 9-17) busily creating egg designs and that year the group won loads of ribbons at the State Fair.

That was twelve years ago, and although Donna still serves as Poultry Superintendent of the Wisconsin State Fair each summer, she has passed along her 4-H responsibilities to others.

Her heart remains in teaching, however, and she shares her special techniques and skills with others through television programs, schools, youth groups, women's clubs and seminars across the country.

Donna's studio in her home is where she designs and produces her egg creations under the label "Eggs Prima Donna." (See photo opposite.)

"A friend was working with a decoupaged egg and had already spent hours on her creation," Donna recalls. "She was painting the background when, for some reason, she stuck her whole thumb right on the front of the egg and smeared it terribly. She was about to throw it away, but I begged her to give it to me.

"I sat for days and tried to figure out how to salvage that awful mess. I had taken some art lessons years earlier and dug out my pastel chalks. With a dry brush, I began dabbing colors on the damaged area. By blending and shading the tones, I eventually completely disguised the smudged place. I covered the egg with a few coats of finish and it was beautiful!"

Her friend was delighted, and Donna had invented a new technique in egg decor. Refining the pastel chalk technique and combining it with decoupage using old-fashioned china prints, Donna creates eggs with the mellow and subtle tones of antique porcelain plates. These beautiful masterpieces are displayed on small brass stands created by Donna's husband in his metal shop.

Donna says the eggs aren't difficult to make, although they require patience and close attention to detail. Beginning artists will find that few supplies are necessary and initial expense is minimal.

And what if you ruin the egg, or the dog eats it?

"You need to remember," says Donna with a smile, "it's only an egg. There are plenty more where that one came from!"

Pamela Kennedy

Photo opposite
EGGS PRIMA DONNA
Donna Marie Runge
(Photo, Gerald Koser)

Editor's Note: For a copy of "Eggs Prima Donna" instructions, send a self-addressed, stamped envelope to "Eggs Prima Donna," P.O. Box 1101, Milwaukee, Wisconsin, 53201.

Easter Goodies

"That basket that you're carrying, my friend,
Suggests that this is not a social call;
I bet you have some coins you'd like to spend —
I would be very glad to show you all
The lovely things I have to sell today
(These are the nicest Easter gifts, you'll see):
Now, how about this colored egg display,
Might there be one that suits you to a tee?
Perhaps, a tiny yellow baby chick
Is more the kind of gift you'd like to buy;
Or could these jelly beans just do the trick?
There are so many flavors you might try."
    The little girl smiled shyly, then did tell
    Of bunnies in her bag she wished to sell.

Amanda Barrickman

Easter Desserts

Easter Eggnog Pie

1 envelope unflavored gelatin
¼ cup cold water
2 eggs, separated
½ cup sugar
¼ teaspoon salt
1 cup milk
1½ teaspoons rum extract

¼ teaspoon nutmeg
1½ cups heavy cream
1 9" pie shell, baked
½ cup heavy cream for garnish
¼ cup shredded white coconut
Green food coloring
Small jelly beans

Soften gelatin in cold water in small bowl; set aside. Combine 2 egg yolks, ¼ cup of the sugar, salt, and milk in heavy saucepan. Cook over low heat, stirring constantly until custard thickens slightly; do not boil. Remove from heat. Stir in gelatin, rum extract, and nutmeg. Cool at room temperature 5 minutes; refrigerate until custard thickens slightly (about 10 minutes). Whip 1½ cups heavy cream; fold into custard. Beat 2 egg whites in small mixing bowl, until soft peaks form. Gradually add remaining ¼ cup sugar and continue beating until stiff. Fold into custard. Pour into pie shell. Chill until firm (4 hours or overnight). Just before serving, whip ½ cup heavy cream. Spoon whipped cream into pastry bag fitted with number 2D star-shaped decorator tip; garnish edge of pie with rosettes of whipped cream. Place nests of coconut (tinted with green food coloring) between rosettes. Place a jelly bean in each nest, alternating colors for effect. Makes 8 servings.

Daffodil Cake

1 cup cake flour
1½ cups sugar
1⅓ cups egg whites
¼ teaspoon salt
1¼ teaspoons cream of tartar
½ teaspoon vanilla extract

½ teaspoon almond extract
4 well-beaten egg yolks
2 tablespoons cake flour
1 teaspoon lemon extract
Lemon Icing

Sift 1 cup flour and ½ cup sugar into small bowl; set aside. Beat egg whites until frothy in separate bowl. Add salt and cream of tartar; beat until stiff but still glossy. Add remaining 1 cup sugar a little at a time; fold in thoroughly. Fold in vanilla and almond extract. Sift flour-sugar mixture over top of batter, a little at a time. Fold in gently with a down-over-up motion; divide batter. Blend egg yolks, 2 tablespoons cake flour, and lemon extract together in small bowl; fold into one half of cake batter. Alternately layer the two batters into 10-inch ungreased tube pan. Bake at 325° F. for 1 hour. Invert pan on wire rack to cool cake. Cool at least one hour before icing.

Lemon Icing

1 pound confectioners' sugar
¼ cup milk
¼ cup lemon juice

Yellow food coloring
2 tablespoons confectioners' sugar

Sift 1 pound confectioners' sugar into small mixing bowl. Gradually stir in milk and lemon juice to smooth consistency, thin enough to drizzle down sides of cake. Tint icing pale yellow by adding several drops of food coloring. Pour icing over top of cake and drizzle down the side. Sift 2 tablespoons confectioners' sugar over top of cake.

Photo opposite
EASTER DESSERTS
Gerald Koser

To Spring

O thou with dewy locks, who lookest down
Through the clear windows of the morning, turn
Thine angel eyes upon our western isle,
Which in full choir hails thy approach, O Spring!

The hills tell each other, and the listening
Valleys hear; all our longing eyes are turned
Up to thy bright pavilions: issue forth,
And let thy holy feet visit our clime.

Come o'er the eastern hills, and let our winds
Kiss thy perfumed garments; let us taste
Thy morn and evening breath; scatter thy pearls
Upon our love-sick land that mourns for thee.

William Blake

Spring Calendar

March is a tomboy of carefree air
In old blue jeans with a patch on the knee,
And a romping walk, and a laugh that's free,
And she catches your heart in her tousled hair.

April comes, weeping in rain-drenched sorrow
That turns to flirtation from laughing eyes.
A tease, a temptress, a gay surprise —
Who knows what April will be tomorrow?

May enters with birdsong and ducks on the pond,
With arms full of blossoms, and bees in the clover,
And when May is gone, spring is over, is over;
Spring is behind us, but summer's beyond!

Agnes Ranney

The Waking Year

A Lady red — amid the Hill
Her annual secret keeps!
A Lady white, within the Field
In placid Lily sleeps!

The tidy Breezes, with their Brooms
Sweep vale — and hill — and tree!
Prithee, My pretty Housewives!
Who may expected be?

The Neighbors do not yet suspect!
The Woods exchange a smile!
Orchard, and Buttercup, and Bird —
In such a little while!

And yet, how still the Landscape stands!
How nonchalant the Hedge!
As if the "Resurrection"
Were nothing very strange!

Emily Dickinson

Photo opposite
CALIFORNIA ICE PLANT
Ed Cooper

Readers' Reflections

Spring's Threshold

Tangled traceries of trees
Show delicate hints of green.
Gossamer glints of gladness flit
Like fairies sensed, not seen.

The woodland smiles in sunlight pale
With primrose promise. Hills
Where winter's faltering footsteps fade
Now dream of daffodils.

A stir within me, bringing joy,
(A subtle whispering)
Says I am standing at the door —
The threshold of the spring.

E. Cole Ingle
Mansfield, Ohio

Garden Silhouettes

Outlined against the setting sun
A family garden just begun;
A tree, a man, a quiet plow,
All silhouettes in darkness now;
The man adrift in thoughtful need,
Fulfilled, perhaps, by planting seed.

The earth lies open on the hill
To wind and rain and God's goodwill;
The man, the tree, the quiet plow
Surveying all in silence now;
Grateful, perhaps, for yearly deeds
Of touching earth and planting seeds;
Humbled, perhaps, by what they've done,
A family garden, again, begun.

Barb O'Hara
Rockford, Illinois

Early April

Last night I heard
The wild geese honking.
Daytime had been Springtime
But night brought snow
To the mountains,

Covering everything.
Last night I heard
The wild geese honking —
Questioning.

Alice Fiedler
St. Petersburg, Florida

Editor's Note: Readers are invited to submit poetry, short anecdotes, and humorous reflections on life for possible publication in future *Ideals* issues. Please send xeroxed copies only; manuscripts will not be returned. Writers will receive $10 for each published submission. Send material to "Readers' Reflections," P.O. Box 1101, Milwaukee, Wisconsin 53201.

A New Beginning

This is the beginning of a new day. God has given me this day to use as I will. I can waste it or use it for good. What I do today is very important, because I'm exchanging a day of my life for it. When tomorrow comes, this day will be gone forever, leaving something in its place I have traded for it. I want it to be gain, not loss; good, not evil; success, not failure, in order that I shall not forget the price I paid for it.

Ken Brock
Miami, Florida

Spring Cleaning

Mother Nature arrives with her brushes and brooms
And washes and rinses yesterday's blooms.
She scrubs the gray skies and paints them bright blue,
Then slipcovers the trees in a fresh green hue.

She defrosts the streams that flow over the land,
Then strings the stars on a new velvet band.
She papers the hills in purples so bold,
And shampoos the fields' soft carpets of gold.

She sweeps the winter cobwebs away from the sun,
Then smiles and surveys her labors well done.
She ties back the North wind and fluffs up a cloud —
Then throws back her head and laughs right out loud!

Sylvia Roberts
Escondido, California

Glad Eastertime

So lovely is glad Eastertime
   That comes in springtime dress
To bless our lives with beauty and
   Our hearts with happiness.

A time when birdsong fills the air
   And blossoms bloom so gay;
It is a rainbow-tinted world
   When Easter comes our way.

Beverly J. Anderson
Fort Lauderdale, Florida

Thought
in Spring

I marvel that a man can be
Insensate to a fern, a tree,
A flower growing in the wood,
Or willow fringe where fence posts stood...
How can he doubt the grace of God
When beauty springs from stick or clod?

How can he doubt God's grace who sees
The light, lace-patterned through the trees,
The sun and rain, the fecund earth,
The ancient miracle of birth,
Who knows the wind and clouds, the sight
Of lifting seas and stars at night?

How wise was He, how wise, Who sent
The spring to be His argument!

Revah Summersgill

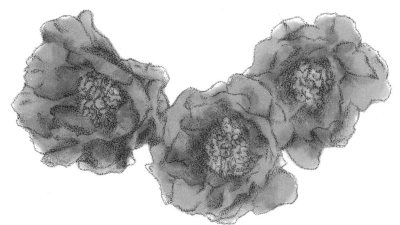

Photo opposite
BEAVERTAIL FLOWERS
Jeff Gnass

Entrance to Jerusalem

And when they came nigh to Jerusalem, unto Bethphage and Bethany, at the mount of Olives, he sendeth forth two of his disciples,

And saith unto them, Go your way into the village over against you: and as soon as ye be entered into it, ye shall find a colt tied, whereon never man sat; loose him, and bring him.

And if any man say unto you, Why do ye this? say ye that the Lord hath need of him; and straightway he will send him hither.

And they went their way, and found the colt tied by the door without in a place where two ways met; and they loose him.

And certain of them that stood there said unto them, What do ye, loosing the colt?

And they said unto them even as Jesus had commanded: and they let them go.

And they brought the colt to Jesus, and cast their garments on him; and he sat upon him.

And many spread their garments in the way: and others cut down branches off the trees, and strawed them in the way.

And they that went before, and they that followed, cried, saying, Hosanna; Blessed is he that cometh in the name of the Lord:

Blessed be the kingdom of our father David, that cometh in the name of the Lord: Hosanna in the highest.

Mark 11: 1-10

The Great Commandment

And one of the scribes came, and having heard them reasoning together, and perceiving that he had answered them well, asked him, Which is the first commandment of all?

And Jesus answered him, The first of all the commandments is, Hear, O Israel; the Lord our God is one Lord:

And thou shalt love the Lord thy God with all thy heart, and with all thy soul, and with all thy mind, and with all thy strength: this is the first commandment.

And the second is like, namely this, Thou shalt love thy neighbour as thyself. There is none other commandment greater than these.

And the scribe said unto him, Well, Master, thou hast said the truth: for there is one God; and there is none other but he:

And to love him with all the heart, and with all the understanding, and with all the soul, and with all the strength, and to love his neighbour as himself, is more than all whole burnt offerings and sacrifices.

And when Jesus saw that he answered discreetly, he said unto him, Thou art not far from the kingdom of God. And no man after that durst ask him any question.

Mark 12: 28-34

And they that went before, and they that followed, cried, saying, Hosanna; Blessed is he that cometh in the name of the Lord.

St. Mark 11:9

The Last Supper

Now when the even was come, he sat down with the twelve.

And as they did eat, he said, Verily I say unto you, that one of you shall betray me.

And they were exceeding sorrowful, and began every one of them to say unto him, Lord, is it I?

And he answered and said, He that dippeth his hand with me in the dish, the same shall betray me.

The Son of man goeth as it is written of him: but woe unto that man by whom the Son of man is betrayed! it had been good for that man if he had not been born.

Then Judas, which betrayed him, answered and said, Master, is it I? He said unto him, Thou hast said.

And as they were eating, Jesus took bread, and blessed it, and brake it, and gave it to the disciples, and said, Take, eat; this is my body.

And he took the cup, and gave thanks, and gave it to them, saying, Drink ye all of it;

For this is my blood of the new testament, which is shed for many for the remission of sins.

But I say unto you, I will not drink henceforth of this fruit of the vine, until that day when I drink it new with you in my Father's kingdom.

Matthew 26: 20-29

Jesus in Gethsemane

And he came out, and went, as he was wont, to the mount of Olives; and his disciples also followed him.

And when he was at the place, he said unto them, Pray that ye enter not into temptation.

And he was withdrawn from them about a stone's cast, and kneeled down, and prayed,

Saying, Father, if thou be willing, remove this cup from me: nevertheless not my will, but thine, be done.

And there appeared an angel unto him from heaven, strengthening him.

And being in an agony he prayed more earnestly: and his sweat was as it were great drops of blood falling down to the ground.

And when he rose up from prayer, and was come to his disciples, he found them sleeping for sorrow,

And said unto them, Why sleep ye? Rise and pray, lest ye enter into temptation.

And while he yet spake, behold a multitude, and he that was called Judas, one of the twelve, went before them, and drew near unto Jesus to kiss him.

But Jesus said unto him, Judas, betrayest thou the Son of man with a kiss?

Luke 22: 39-48

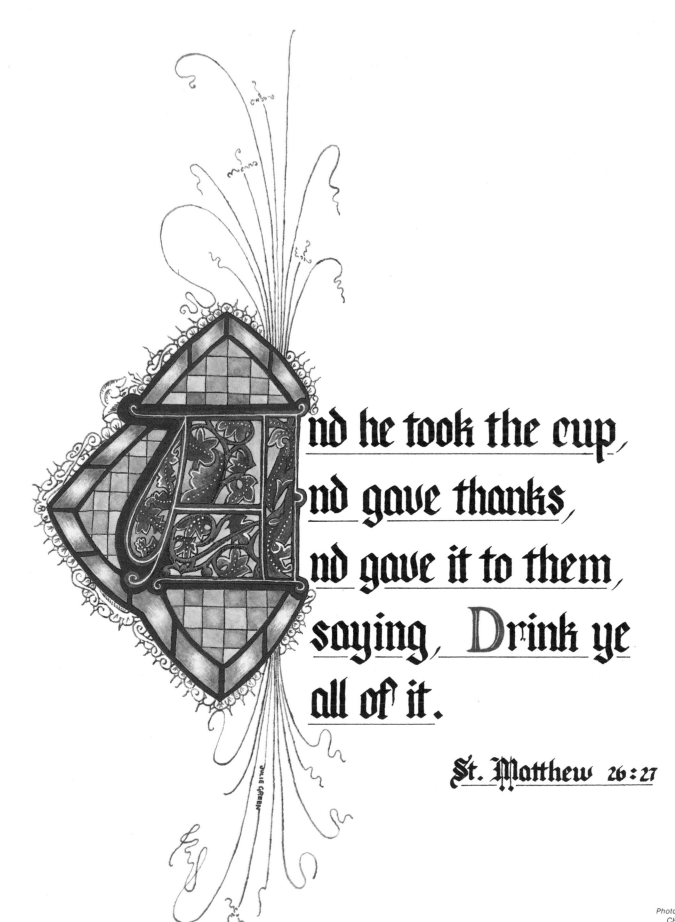

And he took the cup, and gave thanks, and gave it to them, saying, Drink ye all of it.

St. Matthew 26:27

The Crucifixion

And when they were come to the place, which is called Calvary, there they crucified him, and the malefactors, one on the right hand, and the other on the left.

Then said Jesus, Father, forgive them; for they know not what they do. And they parted his raiment, and cast lots.

And the people stood beholding. And the rulers also with them derided him, saying, He saved others; let him save himself, if he be Christ, the chosen of God.

And the soldiers also mocked him, coming to him, and offering him vinegar,

And saying, If thou be the king of the Jews, save thyself.

And a superscription also was written over him in letters of Greek, and Latin, and Hebrew, THIS IS THE KING OF THE JEWS.

And one of the malefactors which were hanged railed on him, saying, If thou be Christ, save thyself and us.

But the other answering rebuked him, saying, Dost not thou fear God, seeing thou art in the same condemnation?

And we indeed justly; for we receive the due reward of our deeds: but this man hath done nothing amiss.

And he said unto Jesus, Lord, remember me when thou comest into thy kingdom.

And Jesus said unto him, Verily I say unto thee, To day shalt thou be with me in paradise.

And it was about the sixth hour, and there was a darkness over all the earth until the ninth hour.

And the sun was darkened, and the veil of the temple was rent in the midst.

And when Jesus had cried with a loud voice, he said, Father, into thy hands I commend my spirit: and having said thus, he gave up the ghost.

Luke 23: 33-46

Jesus said unto her, I am the resurrection, and the life: he that believeth in me, though he were dead, yet shall he live.

St. John 11: 25

The Resurrection

And when the sabbath was past, Mary Magdalene, and Mary the mother of James, and Salome, had bought sweet spices, that they might come and anoint him.

And very early in the morning the first day of the week, they came unto the sepulchre at the rising of the sun.

And they said among themselves, Who shall roll us away the stone from the door of the sepulchre?

And when they looked, they saw that the stone was rolled away: for it was very great.

And entering into the sepulchre, they saw a young man sitting on the right side, clothed in a long white garment; and they were affrighted.

And he saith unto them, Be not affrighted: Ye seek Jesus of Nazareth, which was crucified: he is risen; he is not here: behold the place where they laid him.

But go your way, tell his disciples and Peter that he goeth before you into Galilee: there shall ye see him, as he said unto you.

And they went out quickly, and fled from the sepulchre; for they trembled and were amazed: neither said they any thing to any man; for they were afraid.

Now when Jesus was risen early the first day of the week, he appeared first to Mary Magdalene, out of whom he had cast seven devils.

And she went and told them that had been with him, as they mourned and wept.

And they, when they had heard that he was alive, and had been seen of her, believed not.

After that he appeared in another form unto two of them, as they walked, and went into the country.

And they went and told it unto the residue: neither believed they them.

Afterward he appeared unto the eleven as they sat at meat, and upbraided them with their unbelief and hardness of heart, because they believed not them which had seen him after he was risen.

And he said unto them, Go ye into all the world, and preach the gospel to every creature.

He that believeth and is baptized shall be saved; but he that believeth not shall be damned.

And these signs shall follow them that believe; In my name shall they cast out devils; they shall speak with new tongues;

They shall take up serpents; and if they drink any deadly thing, it shall not hurt them; they shall lay hands on the sick, and they shall recover.

So then after the Lord had spoken unto them, he was received up into heaven, and sat on the right hand of God.

And they went forth, and preached every where, the Lord working with them, and confirming the word with signs following. Amen.

Mark 16: 1-20

Enter into his gates with thanksgiving, and into his courts with praise: be thankful unto him and bless his name.

Psalm 100:4

Photo opposite
AIR FORCE CHAPEL
Colorado Springs
Ed Cooper

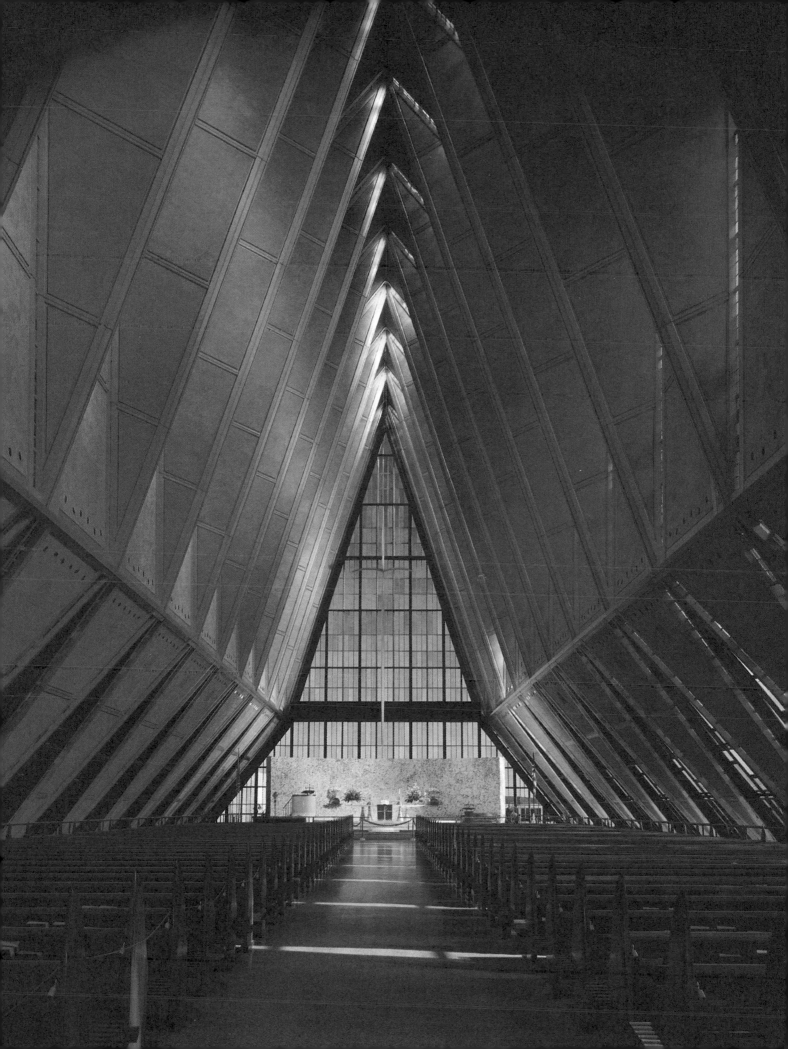

June Masters Bacher

"I've been writing as far back as I can remember," says June Masters Bacher. Beginning at age nine with a social column in her rural Texas hometown paper, she has produced poetry, essays, fiction, and even a series of radio scripts of historical drama. Her inspirational work appears frequently in a variety of denominational and educational publications. Lately, she has been working in a new genre, the pioneer romance, and has had four volumes published.

Wife, mother, and retired teacher, Mrs. Bacher is a woman of faith who gains considerable strength from the beauty of this world. She uses her poetry to capture and reflect her daily thoughts and experiences. "I've always had a deep appreciation for nature — flowers, sunsets, and the like," she says.

April's the Door to Somewhere

April's the door to somewhere
That winter cannot go;
April is filled with sunshine
That fades the winter snow.

April brings sudden showers...
Musical pipes of Pan...
Twisting the awesome storm clouds
Into a colored span.

Oh, April's young and fickle
Because her ways are new,
Making many promises
And keeping but a few.

Perhaps that's why we love her,
Though false hope she may bring:
She opens up a doorway
To somewhere we call spring.

My Heart Remembers Tulips

Each spring I said, "No tulips!"
And yet I'd plant a row,
"Because," I said, "the bulblets
Are simple things to grow."

Each spring I said, "No tulips!"
Though lovely things they are,
A galaxy of color
From cup to sudden star.

They dance along the boardwalk,
My private Milky Way,
A sudden blaze of brilliance —
But only for a day.

But now when spring and summer
Are covered by the snow,
My heart blooms with the tulips
I know I'll always grow.

For tulips bloom forever!
Long after they are gone,
That single day remembered
Blooms on and on and on.

April's Start

These would I keep forever in
The chambers of my heart:
The singing of a robin that
Announces April's start;

A meadow bright and starry-eyed
Where daisies nod and doze
On slender stems grown weary from
Their unaccustomed clothes;

An apple tree with pouting buds
Where bluejays congregate
To bargain for or steal away
Each others' real estate;

The sound of happy children when
Their school lets out for play;
The smell of freshly-spaded sod
On April's first bright day.

An April day is brief, I know,
Yet there's a gentle spell
That lives forever in the heart,
If it is savored well.

One Tiny Bud

The ice has thawed so little yet;
The garden's bogged in mud;
How could it be on one small tree
I see a tiny bud?

I close my eyes and let it bloom
And sense a sheer delight...
One little bud, or dream, or deed
Can bring spring overnight.

The Visit

She tiptoed in so softly
You knew not she was there,
As Spring came for the season
And caught you unaware!

She roused the pussy willows
From winter's sleepy bed;
She deftly groomed the alder
Growing by the garden shed.

She strung a bush with rosebuds
And gave each bird a song —
A melody for Easter
To echo all year long.

And then she fringed the pathway —
A message to impart —
"Forget-Me-Not," God's blossom,
To touch the human heart.

Overleaf
SEAVILLE, New Jersey
Gene Ahrens

The Echoing Green

The Sun does arise,
And make happy the skies;
The merry bells ring
To welcome the spring;
The skylark and thrush,
The birds of the bush,
Sing louder around
To the bells' cheerful sound,
While our sports shall be seen
On the Echoing Green.

Old John, with white hair,
Does laugh away care,
Sitting under the oak,
Among the old folk,
They laugh at our play,

And soon they all say:
"Such, such were the joys
When we all, girls and boys,
In our youth time were seen
On the Echoing Green."

Till the little ones, weary,
No more can be merry;
The sun does descend,
And our sports have an end.
Round the laps of their mothers
Many sisters and brothers,
Like birds in their nest,
Are ready for rest,
And sport no more seen
On the darkening Green.

William Blake

Tulips

The tulips are in bloom again,
   As every passer-by can see —
A lovely sight of red and white
   And bronze and purple pageantry.

Brave warriors of hope are they
   Who nod and sway beneath the sun
And seem to say, "Let come what may,
   Our duty here once more we've done.

"We shall not see the roses bloom
   Nor long outlive the breath of spring
But brave of heart we play our part,
   Each one of us a lovely thing.

"What if in two brief weeks we pale
   And to the changing season bow,
And row by row to death we go?
   We have our share of glory now.

"Gaze on us, weary passer-by,
   Enjoy our beauty while you may,
And like us give, the while you live,
   Your utmost best to every day."

Edgar A. Guest

Painting opposite
EASTER SUNDAY MORNING
Donald Mills

Spring Haiku

Pure simplicity
Marks the arrival of spring —
A pale yellow sky.

A lovely spring day —
Out in the garden sparrows
Are bathing in sand.

Will that very peach
Come floating down the small stream?
The mists of springtime.

Look, a nightingale!
They have lighted on plum-trees
From antiquity.

Tulips

Cup-shapes of yellows and reds
Are springing from long-silent beds;
And bell-shapes of lavender hue
(Intending the spirit to woo)
Are opening slowly to view.

While nodding in fields of new grass,
And blooming in beauty to last
For only the briefest of hours,
Sweet tulips! Your rainbow of flowers
Has brightened this landscape of ours.

Amanda Barrickman

John Slobodnik

My Garden

I made a garden where once were weeds;
I planted tiny colored seeds —
Some zinnias, and some marigolds
That bloom in yellow ruffled folds,

And raindrop seeds of canteloupe
Which came inside an envelope.
They look just like the seeds you see
In melons from the grocery.

I chose a square of vacant ground
Where toothpick grass grew all around,
Beside an oak where sun shines through
With speckled light rays almost blue.

I watered it 'most every day,
And I saw rainbows in the spray.
I watched and watched to see a sprout —
At last the leaves came rushing out.

The marigolds grew lacy tall;
The zinnia leaves are straight and small;
The melon leaf's a lily pad
That bends its head as if it's sad.

The marigolds have opened up;
The melon has a yellow cup;
The zinnias are as bright as beads —
I like a garden more than weeds.

Carrie Watkins

A Comparison

Apple blossoms look like snow,
They're different, though.
Snow falls softly, but it brings
Noisy things:
Sleighs and bells, forts and fights,
Cosy nights.

But apple blossoms when they go,
White and slow,
Quiet all the orchard space,
Till the place
Hushed with falling sweetness seems
Filled with dreams.

John Farrar

Photo opposite
CRABAPPLE BLOSSOMS
Gene Ahrens

Spring Outlook

A man thinks of this time of year as a winter pause, the dawn of spring, a prelude to the richer days of thaw and flowing streams, the open fields. He has watched the osiers along the swamp turn brilliantly red as if to point out the course of the swamp's channel which spring will open, and which the muskrats will use. The willows spread a golden hue against the snow-covered slopes, golden as the light of a late afternoon dipped across the land. The catkins of the pussy willow and the alder are soft and swollen. Winter may still hold the reins of the year in its icy hands, but spring is moving in. A man expects it any day, or any hour. A man knows these very hours are building surely and quietly and gently into a day of music and bloom. He relishes the thought that his hills and woodlands are being prepared for the great awakening, readied for the harrow and the plow and the seed.

The air is filled with expectancy and hope. In the stillness of the morning, a man walks along his creek. He listens to the gurgling sound of water under ice. He listens to the seedpods of the creek bank's giant ash drop with a clicking sound upon the crusted snow. Purple finches are at work among the propeller-like seeds; a man notes the brilliant purple of the finch against the morning sun; he thinks he sees the beauty of the dawn reflected there. Above the pool, a chipmunk hurries over the snow like a yellow streak, like a child drawing a crayon carelessly over a sprawling sheet of white.

The sun spreads its light longer now over an upland farm, and a countryman is receptive to the milder calls and songs. He is receptive to the wood's soft grayness, to the brilliance of the osier and the willow, to the swollen buds of the lilac and the birch and the maple. In this pause before spring, a man warms his outlook for that delightful country hour ushered in over the hills with a robin's carol or a redwing's flute.

Lansing Christman

Expectancy

Incredible! That in a day...an hour,
   Tomorrow...or the next day, it may be,
The thing will happen here...A leaf or flower
   Will startle the young grass, and every tree
Will wear a dim, grey softness, veiled and blurred,
   And there, a swift, blue darting of curved wings
Will scarcely be believed in for a bird,

So long and long expected . . . till it sings.
A little while . . . in one day or in two . . .
   New shapes and colors coming on the air
Like dreams of shapes and colors coming true . . .
   So that I watch, my gaze gone wandering there
Above the listening earth, the swollen bough,
   As though the thing might happen, even now.

David Morton

And Then It Rained

And then it rained, oh, then it rained,
All night, all day, it rained and rained.
And the birds stayed home
And brooded their young.
And the waterfall, roaring,
Was brown with mud.

And then it stopped, oh, then it stopped.
Sun broke through, and the raining stopped.
And the birds came forth
And sang on the posts.
And the waterfall, thinning,
Was bright as glass.

Mark Van Doren

Green Rain

Into the scented woods we'll go,
And see the blackthorn swim in snow.
High above, in the budding leaves,
A brooding dove awakes and grieves;
The glades with mingled music stir,
And wildly laughs the woodpecker.
When blackthorn petals pearl the breeze,
There are the twisted hawthorn trees
Thick-set with buds, as clear and pale
As golden water or green hail —
As if a storm of rain had stood
Enchanted in the thorny wood,
And, hearing fairy voices call,
Hung poised, forgetting how to fall.

Mary Webb

Madelyn Stanchfield Trebilcock

The First Spring Morning

Look! Look! the spring is come:
Oh, feel the gentle air,
That wanders thro' the boughs to burst
The thick buds everywhere!
The birds are glad to see
The high unclouded sun:
Winter is fled away, they sing,
The gay time is begun.

Adown the meadows green
Let us go dance and play,
And look for violets in the lane,
And ramble far away
To gather primroses
That in the woodlands grow,
And hunt for oxlips, or if yet
The blades of bluebells show.

There the old woodman gruff
Hath half the coppice cut,
And weaves the hurdles all day long
Beside his willow hut.
We'll steal on him, and then
Startle him, all with glee
Singing our song of winter fled
And summer soon to be.

Robert Bridges

The Sweet o' the Year

Now the frog, all lean and weak,
   Yawning from his famished sleep,
Water in the ditch doth seek,
   Fast as he can stretch and leap:
      Marshy kingcups burning near,
      Tell him 'tis the sweet o' the year.

Now the ant works up his mound
   In the moldered piny soil,
And above the busy ground
   Takes the joy of earnest toil:
      Dropping pine cones, dry and sere,
      Warn him 'tis the sweet o' the year.

Now the chrysalis on the wall
   Cracks, and out the creature springs,
Raptures in his body small,
   Wonders on his dusty wings:
      Bells and cups, all shining clear,
      Show him 'tis the sweet o' the year.

Now the brown bee, wild and wise,
   Hums abroad, and roves and roams,
Storing in his wealthy thighs

Treasure for the golden combs:
   Dewy buds and blossoms dear
   Whisper 'tis the sweet o' the year.

Now the merry maids so fair
   Weave the wreaths and choose the queen,
Blooming in the open air,
   Like fresh flowers upon the green;
     Spring, in every thought sincere,
     Thrills them with the sweet o' the year.

Now the lads, all quick and gay,
   Whistle to the browsing herds,
Or in the twilight pastures gray
   Learn the use of whispered words:
     First a blush, and then a tear,
     And then a smile, i' the sweet o' the year.

Now the Mayfly and the fish
   Play again from noon to night;
Every breeze begets a wish,
   Every motion means delight:
     Heaven high over heath and mere,
     Crowns with blue the sweet o' the year.

Now all Nature is alive,
   Bird and beetle, man and mole;
Beelike goes the human hive,
   Larklike sings the soaring soul:
     Hearty faith and honest cheer
     Welcome in the sweet o' the year.

George Meredith

Song on a May Morning

Now the bright morning star, Day's harbinger,
Comes dancing from the east, and leads with her
The flowery May, who from her green lap throws
The yellow cowslip and the pale primrose.
   Hail, bounteous May, that dost inspire
   Mirth, and youth, and warm desire!
   Woods and groves are of thy dressing;
   Hill and dale doth boast thy blessing.
Thus we salute thee with our early song,
And welcome thee, and wish thee long.

John Milton

In Early May

O my dear, the world today
Is more lovely than a dream!
Magic hints from far away
Haunt the woodland, and the stream
Murmurs in his rocky bed
Things that never can be said.

Starry dogwood is in flower,
Gleaming through the mystic woods.
It is beauty's perfect hour
In the wild spring solitudes.
Now the orchards in full blow
Shed their petals white as snow.

All the air is honey-sweet
With the lilacs white and red,
Where the blossoming branches meet
In an arbor overhead.
And the laden cherry trees
Murmur with the hum of bees.

All the earth is fairy green,
And the sunlight filmy gold,
Full of ecstasies unseen,
Full of mysteries untold.
Who would not be out-of-door,
Now the spring is here once more!

Bliss Carman

Spring Quiet

Gone were but the winter,
    Come were but the spring,
I would go to a covert
    Where the birds sing.

Where in the whitethorn
    Singeth a thrush,
And a robin sings
    In the holly-bush.

Full of fresh scents
    Are the budding boughs
Arching high over
    A cool green house:

Full of sweet scents
    And whispering air
Which sayeth softly:
    "We spread no snare;

"Here dwell in safety,
    Here dwell alone,
With a clear stream
    And a mossy stone.

"Here the sun shineth
    Most shadily;
Here is heard an echo
    Of the far sea,
    Though far off it be."

Christina Rossetti

Ideals Honors Mothers Everywhere!

Our next issue, Mother's Day Ideals, is a tribute to mothers and daughters of all ages; our inspirational collection of prose and poetry will inspire fond memories that only a mother and daughter can share.

Read about the remarkable life of Anna Reeves Jarvis and her efforts to establish a national Mother's Day observance. Enjoy a fascinating account of one of the most fastidious mothers in nature — the mother robin. Browse among the Readers' Reflections pages where our readers share their own heart-warming thoughts on motherhood.

As always, outstanding color photography captures the beauty of the season. Marvel at the reawakening of nature and the glory of springtime in full bloom.

What better way to say "Happy Mother's Day" than with a gift subscription to Ideals?

ACKNOWLEDGMENTS

TULIPS by Edgar A. Guest reprinted by special permission of Janet Guest Sobell; SPRING'S THRESHOLD by E. Cole Ingle previously published in the *Columbus Citizen/Journal;* THE WIND from A CHILD'S GARDEN OF VERSES, copyright 1917 by Robert Louis Stevenson Charles Scribner's Sons Publishers. Our sincere thanks to the following people whose addresses we were unable to locate: Mrs. Inez Lemke for EASTER; the family of David K. Morton for EXPECTANCY; Revah Summersgill for THOUGHT IN SPRING; and Richie T. Weikel for EASTER BUNNYLAND.